Revision Tips

Rethink Revision

Have you ever taken part in a quiz and thought '*I know this*!', but, despite frantically racking your brain, you just couldn't come up with the answer?

It's very frustrating when this happens, but in a fun situation it doesn't really matter. However, in your GCSE exams, it will be essential that you can recall the relevant information quickly when you need to.

Most students think that revision is about making sure you **know** stuff. Of course, this is important, but it is also about becoming confident that you can **retain** that *stuff* over time and **recall** it quickly when needed.

Revision That Really Works

Experts have discovered that there are two techniques that help with all of these things and consistently produce better results in exams compared to other revision techniques.

Applying these techniques to your GCSE revision will ensure you get better results in your exams and will have all the relevant knowledge at your fingertips when you start studying for further qualifications, like AS and A Levels, or begin work.

It really isn't rocket science either – you simply need to:

- **test yourself** on each topic as many times as possible
- **leave a gap** between the test sessions.

It is most effective if you leave a good period of time between the test sessions, e.g. between a week and a month. The idea is that just as you start to forget the information, you force yourself to recall it again, keeping it fresh in your mind.

Three Essential Revision Tips

1. **Use Your Time Wisely**
   - Allow yourself plenty of time.
   - Try to start revising six months before your exams – it's more effective and less stressful.
   - Your revision time is precious so use it wisely – using the techniques described on this page will ensure you revise effectively and efficiently and get the best results.
   - Don't waste time re-reading the same information over and over again – it's time-consuming and not effective!

2. **Make a Plan**
   - Identify all the topics you need to revise.
   - Plan at least five sessions for each topic.
   - One hour should be ample time to test yourself on the key ideas for a topic.
   - Spread out the practice sessions for each topic – the optimum time to leave between each session is about one month but, if this isn't possible, just make the gaps as big as realistically possible.

3. **Test Yourself**
   - Methods for testing yourself include: quizzes, practice questions, flashcards, past papers, explaining a topic to someone else, etc.
   - Don't worry if you get an answer wrong – provided you check what the correct answer is, you are more likely to get the same or similar questions right in future!

Visit our website for more information about the benefits of these revision techniques and for further guidance on how to plan ahead and make them work for you.

www.collins.co.uk/collinsGCSErevision

Enterprise and Entrepreneurship

1 What does the term 'gap in the market' mean?

.... [1]

2 Which **one** of the following best describes an original idea?

   A An idea that fills a gap in the market to meet customers' needs that no other business is meeting ☐

   B An idea that is obsolete ☐

   C A new version of an old product ☐

   D Providing a cheaper service than competitors ☐ [1]

3 Give an example of how consumer tastes have changed.

.... [1]

4 Why is it important that an entrepreneur is not deterred by the risks of starting a small business?

....

....

.... [3]

5 Give examples of how changes in technology have benefited consumers.

....

....

.... [3]

6 At what stage of a business should an entrepreneur aim to consider potential risks?

.... [1]

Enterprise and Entrepreneurship

7 In business, what is meant by the term 'service'?

.... [1]

8 Which **one** of the following is a benefit of adding value?

A Losing market share ☐

B Independence ☐

C Charging a higher price ☐

D Increased costs ☐ [1]

9 Explain why a business must find out about customer needs.

....

....

.... [3]

10 What does the term 'added value' mean?

....

.... [1]

11 Explain why success means different things to different entrepreneurs.

....

....

.... [3]

12 Why does starting a business present a financial risk for the owner?

....

.... [2]

Spotting a Business Opportunity

1 Why is it important for a business to adapt to meet customer needs?

....

....

.... [3

2 Why is it important for businesses to offer value for money?

....

....

.... [3

3 What are the rewards satisfied customers bring to a business?

....

....

.... [3

4 What is meant by the term 'market research'?

....

.... [1

5 Give **two** benefits of conducting market research.

....

.... [2

6 Give **three** disadvantages of primary research.

....

....

....

.... [3]

7 What does a business need to consider before using market research?

....

....

....

.... [3]

8 Give **three** benefits of using social media to collect market research.

....

....

....

.... [3]

SOCIAL MEDIA

Spotting a Business Opportunity

9. What are the **five** main ways in which a business can segment (divide) its market?

....

....

....

....

....

[5]

10. Give **two** examples of features that can be used on a market map.

....

....

[2

11. What are the **five** ways businesses compete with each other?

....

....

....

....

....

[5

12. Name **one** drawback to a business of competing through customer service.

....

....

[1

1 Outline the meaning of the term 'cash-flow forecast'.

....

.... [2]

2 Outline the meaning of the term 'cash surplus'.

....

.... [2]

3 Daisy Chain is a small florist shop that specialises in fresh locally grown flowers.

a) From the cash-flow statement below, calculate the net cash-flow for February and March.

	February	March
Opening balance	£15 000	
Cash inflow	£12 000	£15 000
Cash outflow	£13 000	£13 500
Closing balance	£14 000	

....

.... [2]

b) What is the opening balance and closing balance for the month of March?

.... [2]

Putting a Business Idea into Practice

4 Daisy Chain has the following figures in June and July.

a) Complete the table with the **five** missing figures.

	June (£)	July (£)
Receipts	27 400	
Raw materials	7300	6900
Fixed costs	2600	
Total costs	9900	9500
Net cash-flow		16 300
Opening balance	21 300	
Closing balance		55 100

[5]

b) Calculate Daisy Chain's total costs for August if their bill for raw materials costs is 10% higher than in July.

....

.... [2]

c) Explain **one** benefit for Daisy Chain of creating a cash-flow forecast.

....

....

.... [3]

d) Explain why cash is vital for Daisy Chain.

....

....

.... [3]

e) Explain how Daisy Chain could benefit from trade credit from its suppliers.

....

....

.... **[3]**

f) Name **one** disadvantage of trade credit for Daisy Chain.

.... **[1]**

g) How might Daisy Chain benefit from arranging an overdraft facility?

....

....

.... **[3]**

h) Name **two** disadvantages for Daisy Chain if it were to use an overdraft facility.

....

.... **[2]**

Making the Business Effective

1 Rebecca is an entrepreneur and wants to open a smoothie bar in her local shopping centre. She has personal savings that she does not want to lose if her business isn't successful. Rebecca has a friend who is eager to be part of the business and is brilliant with accounts.

Would you recommend that Rebecca starts her business as a partnership or as a private limited company?

Explain your answer.

_____

_____

_____

_____

_____

[4

2 What is meant by a sole trader?
Use an example in your answer.

_____

_____

[

Making the Business Effective

3 Explain **two** disadvantages of starting a private limited company.

....

.... [2]

4 What is meant by the term 'business location'?

.... [1]

5 What are the **five** factors that should be considered when a business chooses a location?

....

....

....

....

.... [5]

6 Explain why location is important for a business in the secondary sector.

....

....

.... [2]

7 How has the Internet made an impact on the product element of the marketing mix?

.... [1]

8 How does modifying each element in the marketing mix enable a business to remain competitive?

.... [1]

Making the Business Effective

9 State **one** purpose of promotion.

.... [1]

10 Give **one** reason why an entrepreneur would produce a business plan.

.... [1]

11 How does a business plan help to ensure an entrepreneur has direction?

....

....

.... [3]

12 What information do banks and lenders want to see within a business plan?

....

.... [2]

13 Why don't all businesses need a business plan?

....

.... [2]

Understanding External Influences on Business

1 What is a pressure group?

....

.... [2]

2 Explain **one** way in which the government is a stakeholder in a business.

....

....

.... [3]

3 What are electronic payment systems?

....

.... [2]

4 Give **two** examples of digital communication.

....

.... [2]

5 What does the Health and Safety Act ensure for workers?

.... [1]

6 A consumer is entitled to buy products of satisfactory quality.
What does 'satisfactory quality' mean?

.... [2]

7 What are the benefits to the economy of high levels of employment?

....

....

.... [3]

Understanding External Influences on Business

8 Explain how a business can benefit from a recession when recruiting staff.

_____

_____

_____

_____   [3]

9 What are interest rates?

_____

_____   [2]

10 What is the role of the Advertising Standards Authority (ASA)?

_____

_____   [2]

11 When interest rates increase, what tends to happen to consumer spending, and why?

_____

_____

_____   [3]

12 What does the acronym SPICED stand for?

_____   [1]

Growing the Business

1 Explain **one** benefit for a business of it growing organically.

....

....

.... [3]

2 What does the term 'takeover' mean?

....

.... [2]

3 List **three** disadvantages of selling assets as a way of raising finance for a business.

....

....

....

.... [3]

4 Give an example of when technology has changed the aims and objectives of a business.

.... [1]

5 Give an example of when a business may change the size of its workforce as a method of achieving its objectives.

.... [1]

6 What is a Multinational Company (MNC)?

.... [1]

7 What is a tariff?

....

.... [2]

Growing the Business

8 How has globalisation helped e-commerce?

....

.... [2

9 What is the meaning of the term 'boycott'?

.... [1

10 What is the meaning of the term 'trade off'?
Give an example.

.... [1

Making Marketing Decisions

1 What is the name given to the element of the design mix that refers to the amount a business spends on producing a product?

.... [1]

2 Why may businesses not make a profit during the introduction stage of the product life cycle?

....

....

....

.... [4]

3 How does operating in a competitive environment impact the pricing decisions of a business?

....

.... [1]

4 How will a business price a product with little differentiation?

.... [1]

5 How do businesses make decisions on the most appropriate promotion strategy?

....

.... [2]

6 Give an example of a special offer for a mass market product.

.... [1]

7 Explain how retailers get products to customers.

....

.... [2]

Making Marketing Decisions

8 Explain **one** benefit e-tailers bring to customers.

....

....

.... [3]

9 Give an example of how a business uses place to gain a competitive advantage.

....

.... [1]

10 Explain how the promotion element of the marketing mix influences product.

....

....

.... [3]

11 What are the **five** factors that will influence a business achieving an integrated marketing mix?

....

....

....

....

.... [5]

12 How can a business use price to gain a competitive advantage?

.... [1]

Making Operational Decisions

1 Explain the job production process.

_____

_____ [2]

2 Explain **one** disadvantage of flow production.

_____

_____

_____ [2]

3 How does batch production achieve lower unit costs for businesses?

_____

_____ [2]

4 What is just in time stock control?

_____

_____

_____ [3]

5 What is the impact on a business of having too little stock?

_____

_____ [2]

6 Why is quality an important factor when choosing a supplier?

_____

_____ [2]

Making Operational Decisions

7 What is the difference between quality control and quality assurance?

....

....

.... [2]

8 How do effective quality management systems reduce the cost of production?

....

.... [2]

9 How do customer expectations influence the quality standards businesses set?

....

....

.... [3]

10 How can sales people help customers to make good purchasing choices?

....

.... [2]

11 Why is customer feedback an important part of the sales process?

....

....

.... [2]

12 Outline **one** way a business benefits from offering good customer service.

....

.... [1]

Making Financial Decisions

1 What are direct costs?

_____

_____ [1]

2 What is the formula for gross profit?

_____ [1]

3 What is the formula for net profit/loss?

_____ [1]

4 Pepper Pizzas have monthly fixed costs of £930 and variable costs of £1.80 per pizza. The selling price of each pizza is £8.

Calculate the net profit or loss that Pepper Pizza will make if it sells the entire stock of 400 pizzas in one week.

Show your workings and the formula used.

_____

_____

_____

_____ [3]

Making Financial Decisions

5 Why are profit and profitability not the same thing?

....

....

[2

6 What would a low gross profit margin indicate to a business?

....

....

[1

7 What does the calculation 'average rate of return' (ARR) show an investor?

....

....

[2

8 What is the formula for average rate of return (ARR)?

....

[1

9 What is financial data?

....

[1

10 Suggest **two** ways financial data can be used.

....

....

[1

Making Human Resource Decisions

1 Name a disadvantage of a business with a centralised organisation.

.... [1]

2 Name **two** benefits to a business of effective communication.

....

.... [1]

3 What are flexible working hours?

.... [1]

4 What are supervisors?

.... [1]

5 Name **two** methods a business could use to advertise an internal job.

....

.... [2]

6 What does a CV show?

.... [1]

7 What could be a benefit of a business issuing application forms for applicants to complete, rather than asking for CVs?

....

....
[2]

8 Identify **one** advantage of informal training.

....
[1

9 Why might a business want to train and develop staff?

....
[1

10 When would an employee receive commission?

....
[1

11 What is job rotation?

....

....
[1

Collins

GCSE Edexcel Business
Paper 1: Investigating small business

Time: 1 hour 30 minutes

Instructions

- Use **black** ink or black ball-point pen.
- **Fill in the boxes** at the bottom of this page.
- There are **three** sections in this paper.
- Answer **all** questions. You must answer the questions in the spaces provided.
- Calculators may be used.
- You are advised to **show all your working out** with **your answer clearly shown** at **the end**.

Information

- The total mark for this paper is 90.
- The marks for **each** question are shown in brackets – **use this as a guide as to how much time you should spend on each question**.

Advice

- You must read the questions provided with care before attempting to answer.
- Make every attempt to answer all questions provided.
- If you have time, check your answers.

Section A

Answer ALL questions.
Write your answers in the spaces provided.

Some questions must be answered with a cross in a box ☒. If you change your mind about an answer, put a line through the box ☒ and then mark your new answer with a cross ☒.

---

0 1 **(a)** Which **one** of the following is an example of a cash inflow?

Select **one** answer. (1)

☐ **A** Sales

☐ **B** Wages

☐ **C** Loan repayments

☐ **D** Stock

(b) Which **one** of the following is not an example of primary research?

Select **one** answer. (1)

☐ **A** Survey

☐ **B** Focus group

☐ **C** Newspaper articles

☐ **D** Interview

(c) Explain **one** benefit to a business of having effective customer service. (3)

....

....

....

....

....

(d) Explain **one** advantage of having limited liability. (3)

....

....

....

....

....

(Total for Question 1 = 8 marks)

0 2 **(a)** What is implementing a new product into an already existing market called?

Select **one** answer. (1)

☐ **A** Innovation

☐ **B** Entrepreneurship

☐ **C** Enterprise

☐ **D** Invention

(b) Which **two** of the following are examples of goods?

Select **two** answers. (2)

☐ **A** Mobile phone

☐ **B** Haircut

☐ **C** Doctors appointment

☐ **D** Suit

☐ **E** Bus journey

The cash-flow forecast for a small business is shown below.

(c) Complete the **five** missing figures in the table. (5)

	November (£)	December (£)
Total receipts	18400	
Stock	7050	10000
Fixed costs	3200	3200
Total payments	10250	
Net cash-flow		7000
Opening balance	5400	13550
Closing balance		

(d) Explain **one** method a business could use to add value to a chocolate bar. (3)

....

....

....

....

....

....

(e) Which of the following is most likely to increase a business's profit?

Select **one** answer. (1)

☐ **A** Lower stock costs

☐ **B** Fewer customers

☐ **C** Higher labour costs

☐ **D** Lower productivity

(Total for Question 2 = 12 marks)

Practice Exam Paper 1

0 3 **(a)** Which **one** of the following sources of long-term finance is suitable for a private limited company? (1)

- [ ] **A** Trade credit
- [ ] **B** Overdraft
- [ ] **C** Factoring
- [ ] **D** Share capital

(b) Using the information below calculate the total cost for the small business. Ensure you show any relevant workings. (2)

Quantity sold: 500

Fixed costs: £2000

Variable costs per unit: £1.50

(c) Explain **one** possible conflict of interest between a customer and the shareholders of a business. (3)

(d) Explain **one** advantage to customers of a competitive market. (3)

_____

_____

_____

_____

(e) Justify what a business must consider when deciding upon the prices offered for their products. (6)

_____

_____

_____

_____

_____

_____

_____

_____

_____

_____

(Total for Question 3 = 15 marks)

TOTAL FOR SECTION A = 35 MARKS

Section B

Answer ALL questions.
Write your answers in the spaces provided.

Read the text below carefully then answer Questions 4, 5 and 6.

Peter Harris owns and runs a shop called Harris's Celebrations, which sells cards for various occasions including birthdays, weddings and religious festivals. His shop is located in a busy town centre with excellent transport links. The cards are considered to be high-quality with unique designs and materials used to make the products.

The business has been running for eight months and the revenue has steadily increased month on month. Customers are travelling from various locations to purchase the cards thanks to the unique selling point of the products. Due to this, during peak holiday seasons such as Christmas the store becomes very busy and customers have to form large queues in order to purchase the cards from Peter.

A combination of high demand and an inability to cope with the number of customers in the store is making Peter consider expanding his business and setting up a website so that customers can purchase the products without visiting the store. The website would also allow the ability to see the full range of products offered by Harris's Celebrations.

One customer mentioned "The quality of the cards is fantastic. I have yet to find another card company with as high-quality cards as Harris's Celebrations. However, the experience of the store is horrible during peak times because you can hardly move in the store, as it gets extremely busy."

0 4 **(a)** Outline **one** method of primary research Peter could use to help gather information about his customers. (2)

_____

_____

_____

_____

(b) Analyse the impact on Harris's Celebrations of Peter opening up a website to help cope with demand for the cards in his store. (6)

_____

_____

_____

_____

_____

_____

_____

_____

_____

_____

_____

_____

(Total for Question 4 = 8 marks)

0 5 **(a)** Outline **one** benefit of having high-quality cards in Peter's store. (2)

....

....

....

....

To create the website, it is going to cost £5000. Unfortunately for Peter he does not have this money and will need to borrow the money from a bank. He will pay the loan over two years and will have a monthly repayment of £225.

(b) Calculate the total interest Peter will have to pay for the loan.
Show your workings. (2)

....

....

....

....

(c) Assess whether Peter should use a bank loan to fund his new website for the business. **(6)**

....

....

....

....

....

....

....

....

....

....

....

(Total for Question 5 = 10 marks)

0 6 Peter has fixed costs of £10 000. His selling price is £3 and his variable cost per unit is £1.

(a) Calculate the break-even point. (3)

Peter is going to consider **two** options to increase the revenue for his business.

Option 1: Increased advertisement

Option 2: Reduce prices

(b) Justify which of these options Peter should implement. (9)

(Total for Question 6 = 12 marks)

TOTAL FOR SECTION B = 30 MARKS

Section C

Answer ALL questions.
Write your answers in the spaces provided.

Courtney works in an ice-cream shop in his local area. He is highly talented at making ice-cream and has created many innovative flavours; ingredients Courtney regularly uses include milk, sugar, vegetable oil, salt, cocoa butter and almonds. After working in the shop for several years, he considers starting his own ice-cream shop. Courtney then conducts market research and finds that ice-cream shops have become increasingly popular.

The market is already very competitive, with three main businesses in the local area. However, Courtney has spotted a gap in the market offering low-calorie ice-cream that is of a higher quality than his competitors. Courtney is looking to charge £4 per ice-cream, which is slightly more expensive than his competitors, who all charge £3.75. His research indicates that customers are demanding more sweet treats that are low in calories; this demand is not being met by the existing competition.

Courtney has worked his way up in the business he works for and is currently the store manager. He would be able to raise a significant amount of money to start up his business but would still need a loan. As ice-cream is a luxury item, Courtney is worried that a downturn in the economy may reduce the number of ice-cream sales.

---

0 7 (a) State **one** element of the marketing mix. (1)

....

(b) State **one** variable cost an ice-cream maker may have and explain how this might change throughout the year. (3)

....

....

....

....

(c) Discuss whether Courtney should start his business as a sole trader instead of a private limited company. **(9)**

(d) Using the information provided, evaluate whether Courtney is right to pursue the idea of his business. **(12)**

_____

_____

_____

_____

_____

_____

_____

_____

_____

_____

_____

_____

_____

_____

_____

(Total for Question 7 = 25 marks)

TOTAL FOR SECTION C = 25 MARKS

TOTAL FOR PAPER = 90 MARKS

Collins

GCSE Edexcel Business
Paper 2: Building a business

Time: 1 hour 30 minutes

Instructions

- Use **black** ink or black ball-point pen.
- **Fill in the boxes** at the bottom of this page.
- There are **three** sections in this paper.
- Answer **all** questions. You must answer the questions in the spaces provided.
- Calculators may be used.
- You are advised to **show all your working** with **your answer clearly shown** at **the end**.

Information

- The maximum mark for this paper is 90.
- The marks for **each** question are shown in brackets – **use this as a guide as to how much time you should spend on each question.**

Advice

- You must read the questions provided with care before attempting to answer.
- Make every attempt to answer all questions provided.
- If you have time, check your answers.

Section A

Answer ALL questions.
Write your answers in the spaces provided.

Some questions must be answered with a cross in a box ☒. If you change your mind about an answer, put a line through the box ☒ and then mark your new answer with a cross ☒.

---

0 1 **(a)** Which **one** of the following is not an element of the marketing mix?

Select **one** answer. **(1)**

☐ **A** Profit

☐ **B** Place

☐ **C** Price

☐ **D** Promotion

(b) Which **one** of the following is the last stage of the product life cycle?

Select **one** answer. **(1)**

☐ **A** Decline

☐ **B** Growth

☐ **C** Maturity

☐ **D** Saturation

(c) Explain **one** benefit to a business of having an effective design mix. **(3)**

....

....

....

....

(d) Explain **one** advantage of on-the-job training. **(3)**

....

....

....

....

(Total for Question 1 = 8 marks)

0 2 **(a)** Which **two** of these is not a feature of a public limited company? (2)

Select **two** answers.

- [ ] **A** Limited liability
- [ ] **B** Owners are called shareholders
- [ ] **C** Owners receive dividends
- [ ] **D** Accounts do not have to be displayed to the public
- [ ] **E** Unlimited liability

(b) Which **two** of the following are examples of quality assurance?

Select **two** answers. (2)

- [ ] **A** Quality is checked at every stage of production
- [ ] **B** Quality is checked at the end of the production
- [ ] **C** Quality is everyone's responsibility
- [ ] **D** Only a small amount of defected products
- [ ] **E** High quality products

The table below contains financial information about a business.

Sales	£220 000
Cost of sales	£120 000
Gross profit	£100 000
Overheads	£45 000
Net profit	£55 000

(c) Calculate the net profit margin for the business.
You are recommended to show your workings. (2)

(d) Explain **one** barrier to communication a business may face. (3)

....

....

....

....

....

(e) Explain **one** disadvantage of holding higher levels of buffer stock. (3)

....

....

....

....

(Total for Question 2 = 12 marks)

0 3 (a) Which **one** of the following is an example of an external source of finance? (1)

Select **one** answer.

☐ **A** Personal savings

☐ **B** Loan

☐ **C** Retained profit

☐ **D** Selling assets

(b) Using the information below, calculate the total revenue for two months for the following business.

Ensure you show any relevant workings. (2)

Selling price of product: £50

Month	Sales volume
January	200
February	300

....

....

....

....

(c) Explain **one** reason why a shop selling cars may pay its workers commission. (3)

....

....

....

....

....

(d) Explain **one** benefit of a motivated workforce. (3)

....

....

....

....

(e) Discuss the benefits to the business of using a hierarchical organisational structure. (6)

....

....

....

....

....

....

....

....

....

....

(Total for Question 3 = 15 marks)

TOTAL FOR SECTION A = 35 MARKS

Section B

Answer ALL questions.
Write your answers in the spaces provided.

Read the text below carefully then answer Questions 4, 5 and 6.

Shaketastic is an established British private limited company that has stores in several London locations. Shaketastic has dessert lounges that offer a wide product range including milkshakes, fruit juices, smoothies and cakes, which use high-quality ingredients. The products are manufactured using fresh produce made directly in front of the customer. The customers are able to customise the products to their requirements, selecting ingredients they would like in their milkshake or smoothie. Shaketastic also produces milkshakes using popular chocolate flavours such as Snickers, Nutella and Oreos, which are instantly recognisable by customers.

Shaketastic also has a mobile phone application where customers are able to order products and have them delivered to their door. Shaketastic also uses social media through Instagram and Twitter to promote the company and the products on offer.

0 4 (a) Outline **one** impact of using social media to promote the products. (2)

....

....

....

....

(b) Analyse the impact of Shaketastic charging a higher price for its products. **(6)**

....

....

....

....

....

....

....

....

....

....

....

(Total for Question 4 = 8 marks)

0 5 **(a)** Outline **one** benefit of using brand names in the milkshakes Shaketastic sell to their customers. **(2)**

_____

_____

_____

_____

(b) Outline **one** limitation of higher buffer stock for Shaketastic. **(2)**

_____

_____

_____

_____

(c) Assess what type of production method Shaketastic should use in order to produce their milkshakes. **(6)**

_____

_____

_____

_____

_____

_____

_____

_____

_____

(Total for Question 5 = 10 marks)

0 6 **(a)** State the formula for calculating total cost. (1)

....

(b) Outline **one** possible limitation of Shaketastic delivering products to
its customers. (2)

....

....

....

There are two options to increase profit for Shaketastic.

Option 1: Offer a wider range of products

Option 2: Order cheaper raw materials

(c) Justify which of these options Shaketastic should implement. (9)

....

....

....

....

....

....

....

....

....

(Total for Question 6 = 12 marks)

TOTAL FOR SECTION B = 30 MARKS

Section C

Answer ALL questions.
Write your answers in the spaces provided.

Tesco has recently recorded its greatest loss in the UK. Tesco has removed 5000 head office and store management jobs as a result of its poor performance. It has also closed 43 stores, resulting in 2500 job losses. Analysts have suggested that Tesco let its prices rise too highly and allowed shopfloor standards to fall. One of the reasons for Tesco's decline is that customers have turned to discounters Aldi and Lidl who offer much more competitive prices, with customers seeing little difference in the quality of the products.

However, some customers are coming back to Tesco since it recently cut its prices and improved store service. Tesco now employs fewer staff in management roles but more staff in stores in order to ensure that customer needs are being met. However, Aldi and Lidl are showing no slow down in growth and have significantly increased their sales and market share.

`0 7` **(a)** Name **one** market segment. (1)

(b) Define the term 'customer'. (1)

(c) Outline **one** benefit of Tesco increasing the quality of its products. (2)

In order to make Tesco more competitive against Lidl and Aldi, it has two options:

Option 1: Employ fewer staff

Option 2: Outsource its production to cheaper manufacturers abroad

(d) Justify which of these options Tesco should implement. (9)

(e) Evaluate to what extent price is the most important element of the marketing mix for Tesco. (12)

(Total for Question 7 = 25 marks)
TOTAL FOR SECTION C = 25 MARKS
TOTAL FOR PAPER = 90 MARKS

Answers

Pages 4–5 Enterprise and Entrepreneurship

1. A gap in the market occurs when there is no business meeting the needs of customers for a particular good or service [1].
2. A [1]
3. **Any one of**: consumers are more health conscious [1], consumers are more environmentally aware [1], there is growing consumer demand for cafes and coffee shops [1].
4. The risks can be reduced by market research [1]. Entrepreneurial characteristics include risk taking [1]. There is a chance the business can be a success [1].
5. **Any three from**: consumers' needs can be met more closely [1], more choice [1], consumers can research different businesses and make a more informed decision before purchasing [1], competitive prices [1], convenience [1].
6. At the development stage [1].
7. Service is a non-physical product; an act carried out for you by someone else for money [1].
8. C [1]
9. A business needs to know what customers want in order to produce goods or services that meet customer needs [1]. Customers will purchase from the business [1], thereby increasing sales and profit [1]. **(1 mark for point made, with a further 2 marks available for explanation.)**
10. Added value is the difference between the cost of producing a good/service (raw materials/labour) and the price that consumers are willing to pay for it [1].
11. Success will depend on the type of business [1], the aims and objectives of the business [1], and the motives of the entrepreneur [1].
12. An owner invests their own money into a business [1]. If a small business is set up as a sole trader or partnership, there is unlimited liability, which means the owner's personal assets can be sold to pay the debts of the business [1].

Pages 6–8 Spotting a Business Opportunity

1. So that the business can target a number of different customers [1]. This ensures that the business is current and on trend [1] and their customers do not go to competitors [1]. **(1 mark for point made, with a further 2 marks available for explanation.)**
2. To ensure that the business has enough customers [1] willing to pay a high enough price [1] to cover costs and make a profit [1]. **(1 mark for point made, with a further 2 marks available for explanation.)**
3. **Any three from**: more sales and revenue [1], leading to more profit [1], good customer reviews [1], repeat purchase/loyal customers [1].
4. The process of collecting information about what consumers want, market trends and competitors [1].
5. **Any two from**: to identify customer needs [1], find a gap in the market that is not being met [1], reduce the risks of running a business, to make better informed decisions [1].
6. Primary research can be expensive [1], time consuming [1] and results may be inaccurate [1].
7. The reliability of the data needs to be considered [1]; if market research is not collected in the correct way and from the right people [1], it can be misleading and unreliable [1]. **(1 mark for point made, with a further 2 marks available for explanation.)**
8. Quick and cheap [1]; Data is collected in real-time and so will be up-to-date [1]; Larger number of respondents [1].
9. Location [1]; Demographics [1]; Lifestyle [1]; Income [1]; Age [1].
10. **Any two from**: price [1], quality [1], range [1], colour [1].
11. Price [1]; Quality [1]; Location [1]; Product range [1]; Customer service [1].

12. Training staff in good customer service can increase training costs [1].

Pages 9–11 Putting a Business Idea into Practice

1. A cash-flow forecast shows when payments are due in and out of a business [1] to help a business plan ahead [1].
2. Cash surplus is when a business has more cash inflows than cash outflows [1]; then there is cash left over after paying bills [1].
3. a) February £12000 – £13000 = -£1000 [1], March £15000 – £13500 = £1500
   b) Opening balance: £14000 [1], closing balance: £15500 [1].
4. a)

	June (£)	July [£]
Receipts	27400	25800 [1]
Raw materials	7300	6900
Fixed costs	2600	2600 [1]
Total costs	9900	9500
Net cash-flow	17500 [1]	16300
Opening balance	21300	38800 [1]
Closing balance	38800 [1]	55100

   b) £6900 × 1.1 = £7590 raw materials [1] plus fixed costs of £2600 = £10190 total costs [1]
   c) **Possible answer**: A cash-flow forecast can help predict cash inflows and outflows [1], which can help Daisy Chain establish whether there is enough cash to pay its bills on time [1] and allow time to raise finance if needed [1].
   Possible answer: A benefit would be to make a comparison between the actual inflows and outflows against the predicted inflows and outflows [1], which will help Daisy Chain highlight the areas where forecasts were inaccurate [1], in order to establish whether the forecast was incorrect, i.e. by being overoptimistic, or if there were unforseen financial circumstances [1].
   Possible answer: A cash-flow forecast can help predict cash inflows and outflows [1], which can help Daisy Chain establish whether there is a surplus of cash [1] that can be invested either in the business or in a savings account [1]. **(1 mark for benefit, with a further 2 marks available for explanation.)**
   d) Daisy Chain will need to ensure there is enough cash in the business to pay its bills on time [1] because if there is insufficient cash in the business, it faces risk of insolvency [1], which could cause the failure of the business [1].
   e) By receiving goods and selling them for cash before it has to pay its suppliers [1]. This would remove the need for Daisy Chain to raise its own capital for the purchase of goods [1] and help net cash-flow [1].
   f) Daisy Chain might not benefit from discounts [1].
   g) An overdraft facility can be arranged before any funds are needed [1] in case Daisy Chain spends all of its cash and needs to borrow from the bank on a short-term basis [1]. Daisy Chain will only pay interest for the amount and time borrowed [1].
   h) The interest rate is high [1] and the bank can stop the overdraft facility at any time [1].

Pages 12–14 Making the Business Effective

1. A private limited company [1]. Rebecca will have limited liability so her personal savings are not at risk if the business is not successful [1]. She is able to sell shares to her friend [1]. Rebecca's friend can help to complete the accounts and paperwork required to submit to Companies House [1].

2. A business owned by one person [1]. Examples include: website designer/photographer/hairdresser [1]. **(Any suitable example will be accepted.)**
3. **Any two from:** Company accounts are available for the public to see [1], lots of administration to get started [1], shares cannot be sold to the public [1].
4. The place where a business operates [1].
5. Nature of the business [1]; Market [1]; Labour [1]; Materials [1]; Competitors [1].
6. Transport links need to be good so that supplies can be delivered easily and quickly [1] and finished products can be distributed [1].
7. Business can find out what customers want using online market research [1]. Businesses can then produce goods and services that meet these needs [1].
8. Modifying each element in the marketing mix allows a business to establish a differentiated good or service [1].
9. **Any one of:** Encourages customers to buy a business's products [1], creates awareness [1], boosts sales [1], builds a brand [1], communicates the features of a product [1].
10. **Any one of:** To borrow money from banks and lenders [1], attract potential investors [1], plan the business out [1], research legal responsibilities [1], reduce the risk of failure [1].
11. Aims and objectives are set out [1] and an entrepreneur can refer to these regularly [1] to ensure they are on track [1].
12. They will want to see forecast revenue, costs and profit [1] to determine if the business can pay back the money borrowed [1].
13. Some entrepreneurs will go with their gut instinct [1] and want to start a business straight away without spending any time putting a plan down on paper [1].

Pages 15–16 **Understanding External Influences on Business**

1. Groups of people who want to ensure businesses and governments act ethically [1] in relation to the environment/animal welfare/human rights [1].
2. **Possible answer:** The government wants businesses to do well so that more people are employed [1], leading to a reduction in unemployment levels [1], thereby reducing the amount of benefits the government has to pay out [1].
   Possible answer: The government receives tax from businesses in the form of corporation tax [1], income tax from employees [1], and VAT from customers who have bought products from the business [1].
   Possible answer: The government is a stakeholder in a business that is successful [1] because the business is producing more products/services [1], thereby contributing to a higher GDP [1]. **(1 mark for benefit, with a further 2 marks available for explanation.)**
3. The electronic ability [1] to transfer money quickly and safely from one bank account to another [1].
4. **Accept two from:** email [1], texts [1], websites [1], social media [1].
5. That workers have the right to work in a safe environment [1].
6. Goods or services shouldn't be faulty or damaged when the consumer receives them [1], and they should last a reasonable length of time [1].
7. The more people work, the more they earn and the more taxes they pay [1]. Also, if workers have money to spend, they demand more goods and services [1], which creates further selling opportunities for businesses [1].
8. In times of high unemployment it can be easier for businesses to recruit good quality staff because there are more unemployed workers looking for jobs [1], which means there are more applicants to choose from [1], allowing a business to recruit the most talented people [1].
9. The cost of borrowing [1] and the reward for saving [1].
10. The ASA tries to ensure that all advertising claims are accurate and true so consumers are not misled [1]. The ASA also deals with advertising complaints from consumers [1].
11. Consumers with borrowing tend to have to pay higher interest charges to banks [1], which means they have less disposable income [1], which results in customers spending less or buying inferior products [1].
12. Strong Pound, Imports Cheap, Exports Dear [1].

Pages 17–18 **Growing the Business**

1. The business can keep its values [1] because it has grown independently without having to compromise its beliefs [1], thereby protecting its brand identity [1].
2. When one large business buys a smaller business [1], which becomes part of the original bigger business [1].
3. It can take a while to sell the assets [1] and also the business may not receive the full cash value it is hoping for [1]. Also, it can look a bit desperate if a business wants to sell assets to raise cash [1].
4. **Any one of:** as a response to new innovation [1], new methods of working with technology [1], consumers using more technology [1], e-commerce selling methods [1], or similar response [1].
5. **Any one of:** seasonal work, e.g. Christmas or summer [1], sudden influx of demand from consumers in response to a successful advertising campaign [1], delayering the workforce if it gets too big [1], or similar response [1].
6. A business that produces and sells in more than one country [1].
7. A tax added onto the selling price of an imported good [1] to make it more expensive to buy in the UK [1].
8. Businesses and customers are able to buy and sell products anywhere in the world [1] now that it is easier to reach them due to digital communication [1].
9. When a consumer boycotts a product or a company the consumer is attempting to influence the behaviour of the company by not giving them any money [1].
10. A compromise between one thing and another [1]. **Possible example:** some businesses chose to use environmentally-friendly raw materials to attract customers but the trade-off is that the costs of the business are higher as a result. **(Any other reasonable example will be accepted.)**

Pages 19–20 **Making Marketing Decisions**

1. Cost [1]
2. Research, design and development costs are high [1] and sales are low as customers are unaware of the product [1]. A lot of money will be spent on promotion during this stage [1]. High costs and low sales mean the business will be making a loss [1].
3. Means a business may have to reduce their prices to remain competitive in the market [1].
4. Prices will be similar to competitors [1].
5. They will consider their market segment [1] and decide how best to reach that market segment [1].
6. **Any one of:** buy-one, get-one free [1], discount on the selling price [1], two-for-one [1].
7. They buy in large amounts from wholesalers or manufacturers [1] and make products available in local shops for customers [1].
8. Convenience [1], as customers can shop at any time from anywhere [1] and do not have to go to a physical shop [1]. **Other benefits:** more choice, delivery saves time for customers, accessibility as customers can shop at any time from anywhere. **(1 mark for benefit, with a further 2 marks available for explanation.)**
9. **Any one of:** dispatching orders quickly [1], various dispatch and delivery options [1], being available in locations and times convenient to customers can provide great customer satisfaction and repeat purchases and lead to possible competitive advantage [1].
10. The life cycle of the product may influence the promotion used for it [1]. Often when a product is new it will require lots of promotion [1], in contrast to the maturity stage when promotion takes place less [1]. **(1 mark for promotion, with a further 2 marks available for explanation.)**

11. The objectives of the business [1]; The market [1]; The size of a business [1]; The competition [1]; The nature of the product [1].
12. Offer a price that is cheaper than competitors [1].

Pages 21–22 **Making Operational Decisions**

1. One individual product is made at a time [1]. Once one product is made, another product can be started [1].
2. **Any one of**: a breakdown in one of the lines [1], impacts the entire production process [1]. Repetitive work [1] leads to low motivation for workers [1]. Not much flexibility [1], so difficult to adapt production lines [1]. Machinery is expensive to buy [1] and assembly lines are expensive to set up [1]. **(1 mark for disadvantage, with a further 1 mark available for explanation.)**
3. Products are made in batches [1], so raw materials or components can be purchased in large quantities, allowing the business to receive discounts, therefore the cost per unit is lower [1].
4. Businesses do not hold any stock [1]. Raw materials and components are ordered in exactly when they are needed [1] and used straight away in the production process [1].
5. A delay in the production process [1] and a business may not be able to meet demand [1].
6. A business needs the best quality raw materials or services [1] for the best price [1].
7. Quality control involves finished products being inspected to see if they meet minimum standards [1]. Quality assurance involves checking for quality during the production process [1].
8. Quality will be high [1], meaning less wastage from defective products [1].
9. Customer expectations differ with different brands [1]. A business will need to research what their customers want [1] and match this to the quality standards that they set [1]. **(1 mark for point made, with a further 2 marks available for explanation.)**
10. By matching a customer's needs [1] to suitable products on offer by the business [1].
11. Good relationships are built if customers receive a response to their feedback [1]. Positive and negative feedback is an effective source of market research for businesses [1].
12. **Any one of**: happy customers [1], more sales [1], a positive working environment [1], good reputation [1], competitive advantage [1].

Pages 23–24 **Making Financial Decisions**

1. Direct costs are costs that are directly linked with the production of the goods or service being produced and sold [1].
2. Gross profit = sales revenue – cost of sales [1]
3. Net profit/loss = gross profit – other operating expenses and interest [1]
4. Revenue – total costs = profit [1]
   Therefore, revenue is 400 × £8 = £3200; Total costs are (400 × £1.80) + £930 = £1650 [1].
   Therefore, net profit is £3200 – £1650 = £1550 [1].
5. Profit is the amount of profit a business has made [1] whereas profitability looks at how good a business is at making a profit [1].
6. The lower the gross profit margin, the more stock a business has to sell to make sustainable profit [1].
7. ARR calculates how much an entrepreneur or investor is getting back on the money invested in a business [1] so they know how profitable their investment is [1].
8. Average annual profit (total profit/no. of years)/cost of investment × 100 [1]
9. Financial data is the past, present and future records of the financial health of a business [1].
10. **Any two from**: to show trends within a business [1], banks will want to see financial data if they are considering a lending proposal [1], investors will want to see financial data if they are considering investing in a business [1].

Pages 25–26 **Making Human Resource Decisions**

1. Centralised organisation can slow communication between the shop-floor and senior management [1].
2. **Any two from**: it can minimise mistakes [1], speed up production [1], improve service [1].
3. When someone works the number of hours they are contracted to work but with more choice over when they work those hours [1].
4. Employees who work with staff and have the authority to delegate work, and to reward and discipline staff [1].
5. **Any two from**: notices in staff rooms [1], emails [1], management recommendation [1], announcements at meetings [1].
6. A CV is a summary of a person's career, education and skills [1].
7. Application forms allow for specific questions to be asked [1] in a format that helps businesses treat all staff equally [1].
8. **Any one of**: useful for teaching staff how to use specific equipment [1], can be tailored to the employee in a familiar setting [1], quick and cheap to arrange [1].
9. **Any one of**: for staff to be able to carry out their roles effectively [1], better quality goods and services [1], more productivity [1], higher levels of motivation [1], to attract new recruits [1], help staff retention [1].
10. Once they have sold something [1].
11. When staff are given short periods of time on various jobs before they move on to other jobs [1].

Pages 27–41 **Exam Paper 1: Investigating small business**

The following marking guidance is relevant to **Question 3 (e)**, **Question 4 (b)** and **Question 5 (c)** in both Exam Paper 1 and Exam Paper 2.

Level	Mark	Descriptor
	0	No gradable material.
1	1–2	• Limited knowledge and understanding shown of relevant business concepts with limited terminology used. • Business information interpreted with limited development of points.
2	3–4	• Mostly correct knowledge and understanding of relevant business concepts shown, including appropriate terminology. • Business information interpreted with developed points but with some errors.
3	5–6	• Accurate knowledge and understanding of business concepts shown, including secure terminology used. • Business information interpreted with a chain of logical arguments.

The following marking guidance is relevant to **Question 6 (b)** and **Question 7 (c)** in Exam Paper 1.
The following marking guidance is relevant to **Question 6 (c)** and **Question 7 (d)** in Exam Paper 2.

Level	Mark	Descriptor
	0	No gradable material.
1	1–3	• Limited application of knowledge and understanding shown of relevant business concepts with limited terminology used. • Business information interpreted with limited development of points. • Simple judgement made with limited justification and with limited evaluation of the choices made.
2	4–6	• Mostly correct application of knowledge and understanding of relevant business concepts, including appropriate terminology.

Level	Mark	Descriptor
		• Business information interpreted with developed points but with some errors. • A judgement is made with justification and relevant evaluation made.
3	7–9	• Accurate application of knowledge and understanding of business concepts shown, including secure terminology used. • Business information interpreted with a chain of logical arguments. • A thorough justification of the chosen judgement is made, based on detailed evaluation.

The following marking guidance is relevant to **Question 7 (d)** in Exam Paper 1 and **Question 7 (e)** in Exam Paper 2.

Level	Mark	Descriptor
	0	No gradable material.
1	1–4	• Limited knowledge and understanding of key terms shown with limited terminology used. • Limited application of knowledge and understanding of relevant business concepts, with limited terminology used. • Business information interpreted with limited development of points. • A simple judgement is made, with limited justification and limited evaluation of choices made.
2	5–8	• Mainly accurate knowledge and understanding with good use of terminology. • Mostly correct application of knowledge and understanding of relevant business concepts, including appropriate terminology. • Business information interpreted with developed points but with some errors. • A judgement made with justification and relevant evaluation.
3	9–12	• Sound knowledge and understanding shown, with accurate terminology used throughout. • Accurate application of knowledge and understanding of business concepts, including secure terminology used. • Business information interpreted with a chain of logical arguments. • A thorough justification of chosen judgement and detailed evaluation made.

Pages 28–33: SECTION A

1. (a) A [1]
   (b) C [1]
   (c) **Possible answer**: A business can benefit from effective customer service because it is likely to generate increased revenue from repeat purchases [1]. As customers enjoy their experience of the business it will encourage them to buy the same products again [1], thus increasing the revenue of the business [1].
   Possible answer: A business will have an improved brand image [1], as customers will enjoy the products they have purchased and increase their perception of the quality of the products offered [1]. They can also use social media to share with other customers their positive experiences, which will improve the business's brand image [1]. (**1 mark for identifying a benefit, with a further 2 marks available for explaining the benefit. Any responses that list more than one benefit with no/limited explanation will gain a maximum of 1 mark.**)

Helpful Tips
For these types of questions only make **one** point and justify your reason. It is not good practice to have two responses as you only get credit for your strongest response.

(d) **Possible answer**: Limited liability decreases the personal risk of the owners [1] for a private limited company. This is due to the fact that the owners are not personally responsible for the debt owed by the business [1]. Thus, the owners can only lose the money invested into the business [1].
Possible answer: The owners are not responsible for the debts of the business [1]. They have a separate legal identity [1] so this means that there is less personal risk to the owners [1]. (**1 mark for identifying an advantage, with a further 2 marks available for explanation. Any responses that list more than one advantage with no/limited explanation will gain a maximum of 1 mark.**)

2. (a) A [1]
   (b) A [1]; D [1]
   (c)

	November (£)	December (£)
Total receipts	18400	20200 [1]
Stock	7050	10000
Fixed costs	3200	3200
Total payments	10250	13200 [1]
Net cash-flow	8150 [1]	7000
Opening balance	5400	13550
Closing balance	13550 [1]	20550 [1]

(**1 mark for each correct figure. Full marks will be awarded for the correct responses even if there is no evidence of workings.**)

(d) **Possible answer**: A business could add value to the chocolate bar by changing the taste [1]. They could do this by adding new ingredients, which can improve the quality of the product [1]. If the quality of the product is higher, customers are willing to pay more for the product [1].
Possible answer: A business could create a unique selling point by using celebrities to advertise the product [1]. This will make the product more distinctive [1], making customers willing to pay more for the product [1]. (**1 mark for identifying a method, with a further 2 marks available for explaining the method. Any responses that list more than one method with no/limited explanation will gain a maximum of 1 mark.**)

(e) A [1]
3. (a) D [1]
   (b) Variable cost = £1.50 × 500 = £750 [1]
   Total cost = fixed cost + variable cost
   £2000 + £750 = £2750 [1] (**The full 2 marks will be awarded for the correct response even if there is no evidence of workings.**)

Helpful Tips
To help avoid errors make sure you understand the difference between variable cost per unit and total variable cost. A number of questions will give you the variable cost per unit and you are required to multiply this by the sales volume.

(c) **Possible answer**: A conflict that can exist between the customer and the shareholder is the price of the products [1]. Customers want the best value for money so want the price to be as low as possible [1]. However, if the prices are very low shareholders are likely to make less profit due to a decrease in revenue [1].
Possible answer: A conflict can exist as the customers want the best quality products so they enjoy their purchase [1]. However, this will be expensive as the firm will have to pay for research and development or more expensive materials [1]. This is likely to decrease the profit of the business due to increased costs [1]. (**1 mark for identifying a suitable conflict, with a further 2 marks available for explanation.**

Any responses that list a conflict with no/limited explanation will gain a maximum of 1 mark.)

(d) **Possible answer**: Customers can benefit from an increased range of products available [1]. As there are many competitors, customers will have greater access to products [1]. This means they have more options to choose the best quality product or one that best suits their needs [1].
Possible answer: Customers can benefit from cheaper prices [1]. As many businesses are competing to make sales they are likely to reduce their prices to attract price-sensitive customers [1]. Thus customers are much more likely to get better value for money for the products they require [1]. (1 mark for identifying an advantage, with a further 2 marks available for explaining the advantage chosen. Any responses that list one advantage with no/limited explanation will gain a maximum of 1 mark.)

(e) The following content is indicative of what the answer requires.
  • Price sensitivity of the customers.
  • The level of competition.
  • If their customers are not price-sensitive then the business will be able to charge a higher price for their products without having a significant impact on sales volume.
  • This might impact the price charged as more competition will force a business to charge lower prices to remain competitive.
  (6 marks are available for this question; see marking table on page 57 for guidance.)

Pages 34–38: SECTION B

4. (a) **Possible answer**: By using a survey [1] Peter will be able to easily analyse trends in the needs of his customers using statistics gained from this research method. This will allow him to gain opinions on a large scale [1].
Possible answer: Through using an interview [1] Peter will be able to identify detailed opinions of his customers to see why they may not be happy with the queuing times [1]. (2 marks for a developed point outlining an appropriate primary research method; a maximum of 1 mark will be awarded if the point is not developed.)

(b) The following content is indicative of what the answer requires.
  • Ordering online means fewer customers need to travel to the store, which will mean the queuing times will be shorter.
  • As queuing times are shorter, this is likely to enhance the experience of the customer, which improves the brand image, as the store/cards are more likely to get positive customer reviews.
  • As customer needs have been improved, this is likely to generate repeat purchases as customers have enjoyed their experience and are likely to buy cards again from the business.
  • The better the brand image, the more likely Harris's Celebrations is to gain new customers due to customers hearing positive reviews of the business.
  (6 marks are available for this question; see marking table on page 57 for guidance.)

5. (a) **Possible answer**: By having high-quality cards Peter has a unique selling point over his competitors [1]. This is likely to result in a positive brand image as customers will see Peter's cards as being better than his competitors' cards [1].
Possible answer: Having high-quality cards can give Peter a competitive advantage [1]. This is likely to result in repeat purchases as customers are more likely to purchase Peter's cards as they are better quality [1]. (2 marks will be awarded for a developed point outlining a benefit; a maximum of 1 mark will be awarded if the point is not developed.)

(b) £225 × 24 = £5400 [1]
£5400 – £5000 = £400 [1]
(You are strongly recommended to show your working.)

(c) The following content is indicative of what the answer requires.
  • A loan would be able to provide the substantial amount of money needed by Peter. Unlike other sources of finance, Peter would not lose any control or ownership of his business by taking out a loan.
  • In the long term a bank loan will cost Peter more than he borrowed in the first place. This means that the fixed costs will increase. Some of Peter's customers may prefer to buy the products in Peter's store, so the business has increased costs without increasing revenue.
  • The bank may want to put security on the loan, which means a greater risk for Peter in case he is unable to pay them back – he would lose his assets or personal possessions.
  • As the fixed costs have increased due to loan repayments, it means that Peter may have to charge higher prices in the long term. This may deter price-sensitive customers from purchasing Peter's products.
  (6 marks are available for this question; see marking table on page 57 for guidance.)

6. (a) Break-even point = fixed cost/contribution per unit [1]
£10 000/(£3 – £1) [1] = 5000 units [1] **(Full marks will be awarded for the correct response even if there is no evidence of workings.)**

(b) The following content is indicative of what the answer requires.
  • Increased advertisement will increase customer awareness of the business.
  • Reduced prices might increase revenue as price-sensitive customers are more likely to buy the cards.
  • This is important as Peter's business is new and he will need to make customers aware of his products in order to increase the shop's customer base.
  • As Peter's business is new, lower prices may encourage customers to buy the products for the first time.
  • Increasing advertising would be a more appropriate option as the more customers are aware of the business, the quicker Peter can increase his revenue from a bigger customer base.
  • Lower prices would be a more appropriate option as customers are more likely to buy the products for the first time if the prices are cheaper, which is more likely to increase revenue than advertising.
  (9 marks are available for this question; see marking table on pages 57–58 for guidance.)

Pages 39–41: SECTION C

7. (a) **Any one of**: product [1], place [1], price [1], promotion [1].
(b) Variable costs, **any one of**: milk, sugar [1], vegetable oil [1], salt [1], cocoa butter [1], almonds [1]. Then, **any two from**: the total cost of sugar is going to increase with output [1]. The more products demanded in the ice-cream shop, the more sugar the business will need to purchase [1]. This will cause the variable cost to rise [1].
(c) The following content is indicative of what the answer requires.
  • If Courtney starts off as a sole trader, he will be able to make all of his own decisions.
  • If Courtney starts off as a private limited company, he will have less personal risk due to having limited liability.
  • He has experience in the industry as a store manager so he should be able to make his own decisions without having to consult others. This in turn means that he gets to keep all the profits that his business will make due to being the sole owner of the business. In a private limited company it is likely that he would have to share the profits amongst the shareholders.
  • If the business fails, Courtney will be personally responsible for all the debts of the business. Ice-cream is a luxury item and is likely to be something customers sacrifice during a downturn in the economy. There are also three already established ice-cream shops, which means that there is a risk that Courtney's business may fail and result in personal financial risk.
  • On balance, opening as a sole trader would be a better option as Courtney has experience and would therefore be able to make his own decisions, resulting in keeping all

the business profit, which would have to be shared in a private limited company.

- Opening as a private limited company would be a better option as Courtney is competing in a market that already has established competitors and is a high risk with regard to downturns in the economy. This means that by having limited liability he will have less personal risk as a private limited company.

(9 marks are available for this question; see marking table on pages 57–58 for guidance.)

(9 marks are available for this question; see marking table on pages 57–58 for guidance.)

Helpful Tips
Make sure you have a clear final judgement at the end of a response that is based on the arguments you have made. Never make a judgement at the beginning of your answer, as you must argue first before making a decision.

(d) The following content is indicative of what the answer requires.

- Courtney has shown himself to be innovative, which is an important entrepreneurial skill for a business to succeed in a competitive market.
- A small business selling ice-cream is likely to suffer if there is a downturn in the economy.
- Courtney has experience of making and selling ice-cream and has conducted market research, gaining a good knowledge of the market. He identified a gap in the market, which current competitors are not filling.
- If there is a downturn, customers are less likely to spend money and in particular on luxury products such as ice-cream.
- Identifying a gap in the market for low-calorie ice-cream creates a unique selling point, which is likely to attract customer demand for this specific type of product.
- In a recession a luxury good such as ice-cream is likely to be sacrificed in spending, resulting in less revenue for Courtney's business.
- Despite having established competition in the market, Courtney has a unique selling point, which is likely to allow the business to succeed, as the target market has clearly identified this as a need to be filled.
- On balance, Courtney's business carries too great a risk as a downturn in the economy will significantly reduce the demand for ice-cream products. Also, there is already competition, meaning Courtney's business will have to try and persuade customers from existing businesses to trial their products.

(12 marks are available for this question; see marking table on page 58 for guidance.)

(12 marks are available for this question; see marking table on page 58 for guidance.)

Pages 42–54 **Exam Paper 2: Building a business**

Pages 43–47: SECTION A

1. (a) A [1]
   (b) A [1]
   (c) **Possible answer**: A business can benefit from having a unique selling point [1] where customers see the product as distinct from the competition [1]. This is likely to generate sales as customers are better able to recognise the product [1]. **Possible answer**: A business can benefit from having a competitive advantage [1], as it is able to offer a product that is higher quality [1] than the competition. This is likely to result in a higher number of sales as customers will prefer the business's product to the competition's product [1]. **(1 mark for identifying a benefit, with 2 further marks available for explaining the benefit. Any responses that list more than one benefit with no/limited explanation will gain a maximum of 1 mark.)**

Helpful Tips
A lot of these types of questions are looking at how a business differentiates from their competitors. Use business terms such as 'unique selling point' and 'competitive advantage' – then refer to how these are likely to encourage increased revenue.

(d) **Possible answer**: An advantage of on-the-job training is that it is more cost effective than any other form of training [1]. This is because existing staff generally train new staff while they are working so the company does not have to pay to train staff externally [1]. This means that costs are lower, which means lower fixed costs [1]. **Possible answer**: An advantage of on-the-job training is that it is more productive [1]. If workers are learning while they are working, they are fulfilling roles in the business that would not be filled if they were learning off site [1]. This shows that a business is able to produce more if workers are learning on the job [1]. **(1 mark for identifying an advantage, with 2 marks available for explaining the advantage. Any responses that list more than one advantage with no/limited explanation will gain a maximum of 1 mark.)**

2. (a) D [1]; E [1]
   (b) A [1]; C [1]
   (c) Net profit margin = net profit/sales × 100 [1]
      £55 000/£220 000 × 100 = 25% [1] **(You will be awarded full marks for the correct response even if there is no evidence of workings.)**

Helpful Tips
Have a clear understanding that net profit is gross profit minus total overheads. The percentage should always be less than the gross profit margin.

(d) **Possible answer**: A barrier to communication is when it is excessive [1]. If an employee receives too much information, it is likely to be forgotten or lost [1]. This means that they may not be able to perform the task to the best of their ability, as they have not gained the information required to complete the task [1]. **Possible answer**: A barrier to communication can be that information may not be interpreted correctly [1]. If an employee is given information verbally, the information may be forgotten [1], which can result in a task being completed incorrectly [1]. **(1 mark for identifying a barrier, with 2 marks available for explaining the barrier. Any responses that list more than one barrier with no/limited explanation will gain a maximum of 1 mark.)**

(e) **Possible answer**: Having higher levels of buffer stock means more storage space is required [1]. If the stock is perishable, it means that it is more likely to be wasted [1]. This means increased costs but no increased revenue for the business [1]. **(1 mark for identifying a suitable disadvantage, with 2 marks available for explaining the disadvantage. Any responses that list more than one disadvantage with no/limited explanation will gain a maximum of 1 mark.)**

Helpful Tips
Always consider the types of stock that a business might hold. Stock that is technological can become obsolete very quickly so it is important that a business does not hold too much stock of this type or they will be unable to sell it in the future.

3. (a) B [1]
   (b) Total revenue = selling price × quantity [1]
      £50 × (200 + 300) = £25 000 [1]

(c) **Possible answer**: It is likely to increase worker motivation as they will be financially rewarded for good performance **[1]**. This means that the business is likely to retain its workers as they are more motivated **[1]**. This in turn will increase the revenue for the business through increased sales **[1]**.
Possible answer: As workers are being paid based on how many sales they produce **[1]** they are likely to work a lot harder. This is likely to result in higher sales as the workers are more effective in their job **[1]**. This means greater revenue for the business **[1]**. **(1 mark for identifying a suitable reason for paying commission, with 2 marks available for explaining the reason chosen. Any responses that list one reason with no/limited explanation will gain a maximum of 1 mark.)**

(d) **Possible answer**: If the workers are motivated then they are likely to be more productive **[1]**. This results in cheaper unit costs for the business **[1]**. This means that the business can charge more competitive prices **[1]**.
Possible answer: If the workers are motivated, they are less likely to leave the business **[1]**. This reduces the costs associated with trying to recruit a new worker and train them **[1]**. This means that the business can charge more competitive prices **[1]**. **(1 mark for identifying a benefit, with 2 marks available for explaining the benefit chosen. Any responses that list one benefit with no/limited explanation will gain a maximum of 1 mark.)**

(e) The following content is indicative of what the answer requires.
- Clear roles and responsibilities for each worker.
- Chances of being promoted up the organisation.
- This means employees are more productive as they know who they report to and what their responsibilities are.
- An employee has clear routes for promotion at work so they can move up the structure. This is likely to increase motivation – employees work harder in order to develop their career.
(6 marks are available for this question; see marking table on page 57 for guidance.)

Pages 48–51: SECTION B

4. (a) **Possible answer**: The use of social media allows the business to create a greater awareness of the brand to its target market **[1]**. As the business is able to reach a much wider range of customers it allows it to promote its products, leading to an increase in revenue **[1]**.
Possible answer: The use of social media is a much cheaper form of promotion over traditional methods such as advertisement **[1]**. The cheaper method of promotion allows variable costs to be lowered, which allows the business to charge more competitive prices **[1]**. **(2 marks will be awarded for a developed point outlining the impact of social media on the promotion of products. A maximum of 1 mark will be awarded if the point is not developed.)**

(b) The following content is indicative of what the answer requires.
- If Shaketastic charges a higher price for its products, it is able to break even more quickly.
- If Shaketastic charges a higher price, it may lose customers if they are price-sensitive.
- This means that Shaketastic does not have to achieve the same sales volume in order to break even. If customers are not price-sensitive, then revenue is likely to increase for the business.
- Customers may no longer see the products as value for money and may turn to rival businesses that offer more competitive prices.
(6 marks are available for this question; see marking table on page 57 for guidance.)

Helpful Tips
Always relate your responses to the case study, as this should influence the judgement you make for this question. Are they established? Do they have a strong brand image? If the business has a strong brand image, customers are more willing to pay a higher price.

5. (a) The use of brand names allows customers to instantly recognise businesses they have previously purchased from **[1]**. This means that they are much more likely to trial the product due to previous positive experiences with these particular brands, e.g. Nutella **[1]**. **(2 marks will be awarded for a developed point outlining an appropriate benefit. Only 1 mark will be awarded if the point is not developed.)**

(b) **Possible answer**: A limitation of higher buffer stock is that the ingredients they purchase are perishable **[1]**. If the stock is not demanded then the stock will be wasted as food will expire and not be used **[1]**.
Possible answer: A limitation of higher buffer stock is that more storage space is required **[1]**. Shaketastic may not have the resources in their stores to hold the stock, particularly as some stock may need to be refrigerated **[1]**. **(2 marks will be awarded for a developed point outlining an appropriate limitation. Only 1 mark will be awarded if the point is not developed.)**

(c) The following content is indicative of what the answer requires.
- Job production may be a preferred method as customers may require customised milkshakes.
- Batch production may be a preferred method for the more popular products as they can be made more quickly, which would reduce queuing times for customers.
- Job production would allow Shaketastic to tailor-make some of the products in order to meet the needs of the customer. The higher the customer satisfaction, the more likely they are to repeat purchase.
- If the queuing times are reduced, customers are more likely to enjoy their experience at Shaketastic. This is likely to result in repeat purchases.
(6 marks are available for this question; see marking table on page 57 for guidance.)

Helpful Tips
For these types of questions there is no one correct answer – only justification. For any point you make you must justify why this would be an appropriate method specifically for the business.

6. (a) Total cost = fixed cost + variable cost **[1]**

(b) As the products are milkshakes/smoothies, they need to be kept at a low temperature **[1]**. This means that Shaketastic need a vehicle that can store these products at this temperature, which can be expensive **[1]**. **(2 marks will be awarded for a developed point outlining an appropriate limitation. Only 1 mark will be awarded if the point is not developed.)**

(c) The following content is indicative of what the answer requires.
- Through offering a wider product range it can create a competitive advantage for the business.
- Ordering cheaper materials would reduce the costs of the business.
- If the customers like the new flavours Shaketastic creates, this would create a unique selling point over rival competitors, attracting more customers to purchase products from Shaketastic.

- This results in lower costs and means the business could charge more competitive prices than its rivals, which will generate more revenue.
- Offering a wider product range is a more appropriate option as it will create a competitive advantage for Shaketastic over their rivals and encourage customers to purchase from the business.
- Ordering cheaper raw materials is a more appropriate option as it will reduce the costs for the business, which means more competitive prices can be offered to give customers greater value for money. The greater the value for money, the more likely it is that customers will repeat purchase, increasing Shaketastic's profit.
  (9 marks are available for this question; see marking table on pages 57–58 for guidance.)

Helpful Tips
You will gain much higher marks if you make fewer points but have more detailed analysis of the points you do make. The more critical you are, the higher the marks. If appropriate, counter-argue your points.

Pages 52–54: SECTION C
7. **(a)** **Any one of**: demographic **[1]**, lifestyle **[1]**, income **[1]**, age **[1]**, location **[1]**.
    (b) A customer is a person that purchases a good or service **[1]**.
    (c) An increase in the quality of Tesco's products means that customers will see Tesco's products as better value for money **[1]**, which will make Tesco more competitive against its rivals Lidl and Aldi **[1]**. **(2 marks for a developed point outlining a benefit. Only 1 mark will be awarded if the point is not developed.)**
    (d) The following content is indicative of what the answer requires.
      - If Tesco employs fewer staff, its labour costs will decrease.
      - If Tesco outsources its product to cheaper manufacturers, its cost of production will decrease.
      - As customers have left Tesco to go to cheaper competitors Aldi and Lidl, if Tesco has lower costs then it is able to offer cheaper prices. This reduces the advantages of Tesco's rivals and encourages those price-sensitive customers who left Tesco to return to Tesco. However, if Tesco has too few staff then its store service might slip as staff might not be able to cope with demand.
      - As Tesco struggles to compete on price, then having lower costs means it is able to offer cheaper prices

to compete with Aldi and Lidl. However, purchasing products from abroad can take longer to transport and these products are at more risk of delivery delays, which can impact on store service.
- On balance, reducing staff is a better option as long as Tesco has enough workers to operate its stores. It would mean that if Tesco was able to meet demand, its labour costs will be lower, meaning it is able to offer cheaper prices to be more competitive against discounter rivals.
- On balance, outsourcing manufacturing abroad will reduce costs, which means that Tesco can still offer the same service as its staff levels are the same but it can also offer cheaper costs via cheap imports. This means Tesco is able to compete with price discounters Aldi and Lidl.
  (9 marks are available for this question; see marking table on pages 57–58 for guidance.)
(e) The following content is indicative of what the answer requires.
  - Price is the only element of the marketing mix that will generate revenue for Tesco.
  - Product may be a more important factor as price is often a reflection of the quality of the products purchased.
  - Tesco clearly has been losing sales due to price, as Tesco initially raised its prices, resulting in customers turning to discounters Lidl and Aldi.
  - If Tesco has higher quality products, such as their Tesco Finest range, customers would be willing to pay more money.
  - Therefore, price has a significant impact on customers, particularly as grocery shopping is a large household expenditure. As Tesco has raised its prices it has made record losses, showing a link between price and profit margins.
  - If customers purchase a poor quality product then they will probably not have a positive experience, which is less likely to result in repeat purchase.
  - Therefore price is the most important element of the marketing mix for Tesco due to the high level of price competition from discounters Lidl and Aldi.
  - On balance, product is a more important element of the marketing mix as customers are unlikely to repeat purchase products that do not meet their customer needs. The higher the quality of products, the more customers are willing to pay for the products.
  (12 marks are available for this question; see marking table on page 58 for guidance.)

Notes

Acknowledgements

The author and publisher are grateful to the copyright holders for permission to use quoted materials and images.

All images © Shutterstock.com

Every effort has been made to trace copyright holders and obtain their permission for the use of copyright material. The author and publisher will gladly receive information enabling them to rectify any error or omission in subsequent editions. All facts are correct at time of going to press.

Published by Collins
An imprint of HarperCollins*Publishers* Ltd
1 London Bridge Street
London SE1 9GF

HarperCollins*Publishers*
Macken House, 39/40 Mayor Street Upper,
Dublin 1, D01 C9W8, Ireland

© HarperCollins*Publishers* Limited 2020

ISBN 9780008326852

Content first published 2017

This edition published 2020

10 9 8 7 6

British Library Cataloguing in Publication Data.

A CIP record of this book is available from the British Library.

Authored by: Stephanie Campbell, Helen Kellaway and Tony Michaelides
Commissioning Editors: Katherine Wilkinson and Charlotte Christensen
Editor: Charlotte Christensen
Project Manager: Jill Laidlaw
Cover Design: Sarah Duxbury and Kevin Robbins
Inside Concept Design: Sarah Duxbury and Paul Oates
Text Design and Layout: Jouve India Private Limited
Production: Lyndsey Rogers
Printed and bound in the UK using 100% Renewable Electricity at CPI Group (UK) Ltd

This book is produced from independently certified FSC™ paper to ensure responsible forest management.

For more information visit: www.harpercollins.co.uk/green